ANCHOR BOOKS

POETIC LICENCE

First published in Great Britain in 1993 by
ANCHOR BOOKS
1-2 Wainman Road, Woodston,
Peterborough, PE2 7BU

Foreword

Anchor Books is a small press, established in 1992, with the aim of promoting readable Poetry to as wide an audience as possible.

We hope to establish an outlet for writers of Poetry who may have struggled to see their work in print.

Following our request in the National Press, we were overwhelmed by the response. The poems presented here have been selected from many entries. Editing proved to be a difficult and daunting task and, as the Editor, the final selection was mine.

The Poems chosen represent a cross-section of styles and content. They have been sent from all over the country, written by young and old alike united in the passion for writing poetry.

I trust this selection will delight and please the authors and all those who enjoy reading poetry.

Contents

Sands of Time

Sand golden sand, flowing through my hand,
like time that escapes us all.
We used to play here.
Content.
For hours on end in granny's backyard we'd sit
Watching the sunset as the shadows grew tall.
What mysteries were to be found?
In spacious ground, granny called garden
We did not know.
But with gun in hand to a faraway land we pursued
to conquer foe.
You were the hero,
    'bang, bang, you're dead!'
But no wound would show,
No blood would flow,
and the villains never died only came back for more.
It was no longer a gentle garden, with beautiful butterfly.
It was a jungle!
Thick with trees, and green upon green,
With villain and murderer unseen,
except to you and me, who defied fear, saved the world
and got home in time for tea.

Paul Bradley

The Miser - an Epitaph

Money the route of *Evil*,
Most powerful as well!
I'd rather be in *Heaven*,
Than rotting down in *Hell*!

Jacqueline Dixon

Hard Slices of Life

To those who knew that constant, gnawing ache
Through once having made a foolish mistake;
Passed a tactless remark; let their tongue slip
Which smashed to bits a good relationship.

To those fate smiled on thus, they made the grade;
On the quick way up lots of friends they made.
But when fate's bright smile changed to a dark frown . . .
Few friends had they on the quicker way down.

To whose who wept, bled and pined, inwardly,
For a rare, true love which could no more be;
Henceforth, out of reach; beheld from afar
As, alas, star-crossed rare, true loves oft are.

To those whose trust was oft betrayed; 'til they
Trusted no one; through which they, sad to say,
Hard as nails became to hide the hurt deep;
And the unshed tears which cried; 'Let us weep.'

To those who asked in the wolf at the door!
Well, 'twas through their own fault that they were poor;
For once they had it all! But lost it; through
Not valuing it; and wasting it, too.

To those straight who through disillusionment
Became bent; to whom love came . . . Heaven sent!
A love which straightened them out just in time . . .
To save them from leading a life of crime.

To those for whom life was bitter and rough
'Til, in despair, they cried: 'I've had enough!
What, on Earth, is it all for?' That sad cry
Is wrung from most of us oft ere we die.

Ward Handforth-Holroyd

My Neighbours

Neighbours are a blessing
My life with theirs entwines
Let me tell a story
About a few of mine.

There's Mrs Scott, from one door up
She cooks and bakes all day
And then comes round the neighbourhood
With scones and cakes on trays.

And then there's Bert, the gardener
His allotment is a treat
He digs and weeds all summer
Then gives me vegetables to eat..

At number ten, the Duncans' live
The husband, wife, two boys
The washing line is always full
With baby clothes and toys.

Across the road lives Mrs Smith
Who hides behind her curtains
She's nosy, always watching
Knows about us all, I'm certain.

Next door to me lives dear old Dave
My mentor and my friend
He's always there to lend a hand
On him I can depend.

As I look around my neighbourhood
I'm happy with my lot
Oh! I forgot to get some milk
Must call on Mrs Scott!

Marjorie Edgar

Within the Depths of Me

I will not let the rot of sore guilt and hatred
consume me.
It will not eat from my flesh
to be the warped master of my destiny.
Its bitter taste will not taint
what I hold true.
Strength is found in an open hand
not in the clenched fist of anger.
The actions of one will be judged
one by one.
Whether for good or for evil our thoughts
are our souls,
they are our Gods.
We are what we believe,
we should believe in what we are.
The greatest thing I have ever done in my life
is to forgive
The wounds deep as they may be
will heal first from within the depths of me.

Steve Winter

A Gale

The wind so quickly changed
From a gentle breeze,
Violently it's blowing
Raging through the trees.
Rushing round the chimney
with an angry roar,
Buffeting the windows
whining at the door.
Such wild gusts have made it
difficult to walk,
Streets are almost empty
no-one stops to talk.

There has been no respite
From the wind all day.
Doing so much damage
Howling on its way.
As dies the sun at dusk
In a darkening sky
Oh that this awesome wind.
Will too, fade and die.

Vera Hardwidge

The Flat Dog

I've got a dog called greedy
And he chases a cat called speedy
His eyes are very beady
When he eats his lunch
And he does this with a munch munch munch
Then he chewed my mummy's hat
And chased the cat right off the mat
He thought he would get a good pat
But instead he got run over and was flat
And that
was the end of my greedy dog.

Guy Sutherland (8)

Huddersfield

In Huddersfield
There's a place called
St George's Square
With proud facade
Of a station so fine, so rare.
A tavern too
Where our townies abound
To hear in Huddersfield
The Mayfair sound.

Our lion so proud and stern
Stands guard high above the square.
Our citizens showed concern
When he went away for repair.

But now he's back
Overlooking our splendid square,
A noble sight
Midst the splendour of civic care.
It's up to us
To not let him down
The symbol of our pride
In Huddersfield town.

Brian Noon

Party Night

It is the night, the special-sparkling neon bright night,
members outshine the decorations, the hall is starry eyed.
Long legged lasses, spiky headed youths, tightly permed
grannies, tightly pressed grandpas, with cigars blazing
and the small orchestra making enough noise to fill the
Albert Hall.

The floor is decorated with streamers, gaiety, balloons as
The Gay Gordons are screeching, whirling, shouting and all
joining in the escapade.
The night is awakening to the occasion and goes scarlet,
now comes the interval. Time passes, and gets hungry, and
thirsty. Beers, lagers, Babychams all mix in abandon with
gin.

Now the jiving, rattling and rolling the swinging to the din.
Grandpa has-a-go whilst Grandma serves sandwiches.
Everyone wants something. To be fed, watered, or loved all
at the same time.
Chairs become beds, as young lovers nibble each other like
grass and you can hear the party still enjoying itself.

The party is tired. The taxis, cars, bikes, feet, shoes
high-heeled, flat footed, or booted, and make for beds,
chairs, sofa or duvets and soon the party is as unconscious
as last year's party.
Nothing had been broken, nothing stolen, on this special
neon star filled, golden party night . . . and it is
dreaming of next year's.

Marjorie Fleur-Oldfield

Yearn

Drifting on the waves of loneliness
Waiting to be found
Searching for answers
To questions unasked
Praying to a silent God
Emptiness surrounds me
Misery scars my soul
Oh for someone to hear, to be
I long until the night comes
Then I am no longer alone
Then darkness embraces me
Fills my heart
I sleep
I do not wish to wake
On another desolate dawn
Don't know how long I've been out here
Don't know who I am any more
Is anyone looking for me
Does anyone care
You'll never find me
I am everywhere.

Steve Evans

Goodbyes

Time comes too soon when we must part,
and say farewell forever.
The pain too great, a cruel fate.
Blind grief and tears at heart.

Or so it seems, unless . . .

Goodbyes must always show the morrow,
to grace each season given.
Like birth and death are one in life,
our joy is one with sorrow.

So fare ye well, we'll meet again.
Another moment beckons.
With boundless love we're blessed we know.
To crown and wound us then.

Peter Schwartz

My Window

Life is a stairway
I must climb every day.
Each step leads upwards,
There is no other way.

Some steps are steep,
But I must not despair.
I'll just ask God to lighten
My burden, with prayers.

My journey has been long
My goal I now see,
For there in the distance,
A window just for me.

I turn and look round
At the top of life's stair,
See the life that I had
With the loved ones I share.

But now I must leave them,
'Tis the end of my fight.
And step through my window
Into God's loving light.

J Ashley-Green

My Little Garden

I love my little garden
Full of beauty rare,
With fragrance sweet and colour true,
For the Peace of God is there.

I love to walk in a garden
With apple blossom fair
For nature's gift gives pleasure
For the Peace of God is there.

I thank God for my little garden
Where flowers grow astir,
A song in the heart is awakened
For the Peace of God is there.

Doris Challis

An Orchestral War

It all started when the grand pianoforte,
Called the great Welsh harp naughty,
The bassoons then made a loud wisecrack,
And the kettle drum called the oboe black.
The French horn joined in the affray,
Saying 'Ooh la la and Cor-vous-Anglaise!'
The clarinet accused the flute of squeaking,
And also claimed the piccolo was cheating!
The euphonium and the B Flat stopped speaking.
'Ho! Ding Dong Bell!' said the xylophone.
The trumpets blared down the trombone's cone!
The viola got hot and soon began to smoulder,
Almost choking poor old Tubby the tuba,
Then the tubular bells started to loudly ring,
But the triangle could only say 'Ting! Ting!'
The double bass called the fiddle, a vile inn,
That made the strings start a terrible din!
The saxophone told the cello where to stick his bow,
Oh, how could they stop it; they did not know?
Then the cymbals came down with a mighty crash,
The musicians, to the exit, they made a dash,
Then the angry conductor too, put his hat on,
But stopped it dead; by throwing down his baton!

Percy Vere

Non sum qualis eram bonae sub regno Cinemae

With a nod to Ernest Dowson

Last night, on television, just after News at Nine,
There fell thy shadow Cinema, shades of the old long syne,
A Film last seen 'twixt kisses and the wine
Gums, and the front row's strange distortion,
Upon my cathode ray tube came to shine
Yes, I have been faithful to thee, Cinema! in my fashion.

All night upon my ear
The old film music beat,
Which once I'd queued up hours for
Out in the drizzled street,
Bringing back the memories of an ancient passion,
And I have been faithful to thee, Cinema, in my fashion.

Attending not thee Cinema, even for Gone With The Wind,
Yet I watched stuff like European Song,
Come Dancing put thy Astaire's out of mind,
I'd half forgotten Scarlet's flaming passion,
In that old film which was quite four hours long.
Still, I have been faithful to thee, Cinema! in my fashion.

I've I looked at game shows and remembered What's My Line,
When Jasper Carrot's over and the late, late films come on,
They cast they shadow Cinema, and 'til dawn the screen is thine,
For all night long the idiot's dim lantern
Displays the works of Houston and Renoir,
And I am faithful to thee, Cinema! in my fashion.

A G Stewart

Lucky me

I wonder if my father thinks of me on Father's Day
I mean the man I've never met
His passion gave me life but I was signed away
And yet I do not fret.

An infant for adoption cannot express a choice
But fate smiled kindly down on me
I heard the tender soft breathing of their voice
And was bound to new parents in a nursery.

My childhood was all wonder and pleasure
We enjoyed our lives to the full
I was given confidence and learned how to use leisure
And how to live by the rules.

They gave me their loving care sometimes through tears
Encouraged learning with guidance and trust
Prepared me for my maturer years
And taught me always to be just.

I can never repay this love and affection
But special days allow me to show
My love and my deep appreciation
For everything they managed to bestow.

On Father's Day I'll be present
With a card a gift and a smile
I'm glad of this day it's a personal day
When a child can give pleasure a while.

I shall spare a thought too for my unknown Dad
Perhaps he does think of me who can say
I should like him to know that my life has been glad
Especially on Father's Day.

John Janes

For Emily Found

Coming home
from holding you
and sharing your first sunset
- even the moon was smiling!

David J Garbutt

The Wood

Not many feet have trod the silent wood . . .
Whose trees have gifted - over years - a carpet soft of leaves
No house or building here has stood . . .
. . . just peace

Peeping through the arms of trees spread wide
Shafts of light - like harp strings - tight . . .
Awaiting to accompany the songs of birds - in flight . . .
. . . just peace

Rarely is there sound - a gentle breeze perhaps
To rustle the leaves and grass . . .
Or an animal - wild - as a twig it snaps . . .

. . . Pray let this peace
not pass!

H W Shawyer

Old Age

Old age is a time that comes to us all.
Whether we like it or not.
You can deny it, defy it, but it wins in the end.
So accept it, it's part of your lot.

It's a time to review the life you have had
The lean times, the glad times, and times that were sad
You remember your school days so long long ago
Those endless hot summers and the cold winter snow.

You smile at the memory of teenage romances
And the latest tunes at the Saturday night dances.
Then came your wedding - your special day.
The smiles and tears and that lovely bouquet.

Your Book of Memories you can browse at your leisure
They will give you a lot of quiet pleasure
And at the end of the book there comes old age.
And you wait for God to turn the next page.

A M Miller

A Distant Light

To cast a weary glance
Upon the ocean blue
A light off in the distance
I watched it shining through.

A lonely figure standing
Just sea and sand and sky
And in my head a pounding
The tears fall from my eyes.

The sea now drawing closer
Sand soft under my feet
The sky is growing darker
My heart how fast it beats.

The water all around me
Into the sand I sink
The sky no longer can I see
No more now do I think.

No lonely figure standing
For that was only I
There is now just the distant light
And sand and sea and sky.

Diane Jones

Sunflower

Sunflower laughing, having fun,
Sunflower dancing in the sun,
Sunflower sad when skies are grey,
Sunflower glad at the break of day,
Sunflower faces always bright,
Sunflower turning until the night,
Around and around from dawn 'til dusk,
Round little faces, turn they must,
Yellow faces, your heart to mend,
When you have a sunflower,
You have a friend.

C J Howland

Untitled

Frankly it's too soon to say
How we react from day to day
When we are young life's all play
Then as teenagers we have a lot to say
Into twenties we sail along. Singing our own sweet song
Bump into thirties we start to look around
Along comes forties with hardly any sound
Sshhh: it's fifties as we walk slower
Now we are sixty and not so nifty with glasses to see
and volume up louder
We guess we are seventies and now reminiscing.
'What happened to all the years that are missing?'
Remember to enjoy things as you go along to make
Life one sweet song.

June Brewer

When I Get Older . . .

When I get older,
I'll be a bird,
I'll fly through the air,
Without a word.

Then I'll be
A chocolate maker,
Next I'll be
The undertaker.

Then I'll be a waitress,
Serving cups of tea.
But a child, at the moment,
Is the right job for me.

Heather Dennison (11)

To a Rose

Ere now your gentle flame danced gracefully
  beneath the sky.
Those deep blush petals, so purely innocent
  and as sweetly shy.
Had unfurled to reveal the tender beauty
  of an angel's art,
With a heavenly sweet perfume had she
  sprinkled your heart.

Your loveliness at morn bejewelled at eventide
  enhanced with rain.
These I'd have captured in painting your graces
  seeking ever in vain.
To portray like charms in sunny hours
  is every artist's quest
Yet her magic touch remains your secret
  while you fade so blest.

Alas! fair rose! those precious petals
  soon must wilt and fall;
Tossing silently on summer breezes,
  wafting softly across the lawn.
Farewell! Red Rose! I now look on sadly
  whilst your glowing ember dies;
Goodbye rose of love how soon are you lost
  to some fairer paradise.

Joyce Nina Pountney

Dad on the Dole

I'm fed up. I'm bored. I'm angry.
Everyone's happy but me.
They're all going off on holidays
To sunbathe and lie by the sea.
My granny is off to Majorca,
My uncle is going to Greece,
He's taking my Great Aunty Gladys
And her spoilt and snotty-nosed niece.
They asked me at first if I wanted to go
But it meant that I'd have to pay
My dad, well he can't afford it
'Coshe's been on the dole since last May.
So the snotty-nosed niece is going
I hope she feels sick on the plane
And finds the hotel is only half built
And the weather just pours down with rain.
Our neighbours will go to Orlando
To see Mickey Mouse and his friends,
The nearest I'll get is to ask my dad
To wear some false ears and pretend.
My mum says I'm naughty for moaning
And casting such gloom and depression
She says that our family can all go away,
Once the country comes out of Recession.

Andrea Mason

Verses

As a child, mouthing verses like 'Gentle Jesus, Meek and Mild',
Or perusing the anthology, somewhat enamoured of wisdom's halo,
Often I would sense a wide expanse of knowledge and the depth
Of feeling I thought experience sedimented in words.

Precious fossils embedded in alien environments, unearthed,
Gave a sensation both edifying and belittling. Structures
Of feelings I would one day live through were showcased in verses.
Never to return to those days. Never, never 'til never no more.

Now a sadder and wiser child. All grown up and words eroded,
Flattened by scirrocos of time. I hate pretensions of depth.
One digs for fool's gold when digging for meaning. Actions,
Read before they're lived. 'Gentle Jesus', now the ungodliest bosh.

Still verse holds a spotlight, now I'm charmed by the *act* of reading.
The project diminished, yet still I can linger in the poet's round.
It is there craft may be found in a more superficial dwelling;
To tell, not to live, but make a life of the telling.

Lyndon Bird

First Impressions

First impressions, what do I see
When people pass by and smile at me
It makes the day when they say hello
What they really feel, we never know.

Then you might see someone with a frown
They pass by with eyes cast down
You think what a misery they must be
Some things happen which we cannot see.

First impressions we should not judge
When you feel sad a smile's hard to budge
Be the first to smile, and say hello
Then you may see a sad face glow.

H D Edwards

It's Peaceful There

There's a world in the sky,
Somewhere way up high
Higher than the clouds
Where there's no noisy chatting crowds.
It's peaceful up there.

That's where we go when we're at the end,
When we haven't got a single friend
We're happier there,
because everything's fair
No wars are there
and people care.

Rose Judeh (10)

Back Home

Today the sun is clear and bright,
And everywhere there's warmth and light,
Familiar sounds float on the air,
As I sit relaxed in my garden chair.
People's voices, children playing,
A bark, an aeroplane overflying.
I've only been gone five days away,
Long enough for any stay, where
outside things are shut away.
I really missed the big green trees
and the rustle of the wind amongst their leaves.
The patio pots with their flowers array -
I remember planting so small in May.
The bright red flags that march across the lawn,
The singing of the birds so loud at dawn.
All these things are part of my day,
Especially the purring of Tigger May.

Yes, it's good to be home!

Irene Healey

Commerce Centre

Morning comes to Commerce Centre,
Hustle, bustle, jostling scene,
In twos and threes and groups we enter,
Broadway House collects its team.

Commissionaire in spacious foyer,
Lifts ascending, workers keen?
Floors first, second, third, the load is lighter,
Broadway House enfolds its team.

To the sales, departments, sundries,
On the phone they give the word,
We are exporters to all countries,
All the countries of the world.

Fax machines, busy humming,
Information, hot off the press,
Replies are pronto, whilst enquiring,
By the way, do you like my dress?

Afternoon and time is slipping,
Quickly through our fingers now,
Dusk is falling, lights are dipping,
Come on folks let's take a bow.

Jostle, hustle, lifts descending,
All pour out, a gladsome scene,
Cheerio, the day is ending,
Broadway House has lost its team.

Teresa Murphy

Untitled

Summer came trees are bowed with rain
Dripping wet
Inky clouds, grey clouds sweeping the
Heavens above
Another drizzle
Downpour
Humid warm
A thunderstorm
Deafening music rolling deep
Giant crescendo dies away
Distant, distant, distant
Sound of muffled drums
Dispersing clouds
Patches blue
Summer sun just breaks through
To hide again behind the clouds
With grey and black tinged with yellow
Summer's here to stay
Drenching wet

W E Roberts

The View

The view from our window is really fine
As I look out, these thoughts are mine
The fields and the brook are always there
In the distance, the farms, and the neighbours we share
In spring there's the flowers, with colours so gay
Children will gather them, to cheer up our day
Little lambs with their mothers, delightful to see
Running races and jumping, as high as can be.

After a winter indoors, though bedded with straw
The cows are all mooing, to be out once more
Now they're fighting and running and prancing around
Delighted to feel, their feet on the ground
In eating the grass, I know they will be
Just filling their udders, with milk for our tea.

Then summer is here, with its warm sunny days
The grass growing tall, for the mower to rage
For haymaking too, it has to be done
And though it's hard work, there's still lots of fun.
The tractors are humming, from morning 'til night
As we bring in the bales, and pack them so tight.

In autumn the corn, and potatoes, too
Fruits are a-ripening to see winter through
For winter it comes, with its mantle of snow
Trees all aglistening, the heavens aglow.
Thus we move through the year, ever-changing the view
'Til Christmas is here, and another year too.

Dora Beswick

My Poem . . .

I went into the baker's shop, I was going to buy a pasty,
Suddenly, two yobs barged in and started acting nasty.
They went up to the manager, the guy who runs the place,
One picked up a custard pie and shoved it in his face.
Then a thought struck me,
I seized a loaf of bread.
I hit the yobbos with it, yeah, I hit them round the head!
PC Astill appeared on the scene,
And said 'Well done, you've caught them both' . . .

So now I am a hero, because I used my loaf!

Matthew Astill (11)

The Evaporated Pond

The pond is dry
Animals *die*
One by one
Trees are dead
Not enough water gets to the surface

People cut down the trees
Not enough oxygen
Not enough food
Mahogany is precious
Animals too.
The ground is dry
Too dry
For anything to grow!

Andrew Banks (10)

Lonely

You're the sunlight, I'm the moon,
You the morning, I past noon,
You're the day and I'm the night,
Suffering in my silent plight.
I wander lonely through my dreams,
A heap of thoughts and unjoined seams,
Worries, memories, happy times,
Mournful bells and joyous chimes,
I think of you, then think of me -
A sad old man with a cup of tea.

Rachel Simpson (13)

Dead City

A crack, a shudder and panic in the midst,
A sudden silence, a man shakes his fist,
A crash of glass, which flies through the air,
A group of people stunned as they stare.
A cry of pain and shock all around,
Some people have fallen to the ground,
Hurt and cut, scratched and in pain,
The IRA have planted a bomb again.

Innocent people blown to the ground,
Police and ambulancemen all around,
The town is cut off, no way to get in,
Another goes off just after ten.
Cutting and hurting people again,
Shattering doors and window frames,
Panic and fear among the crowds,
Dark smoky mists among the clouds.

Blue flashing lights smother the air,
The bomb squad have just arrived in there,
Running around and searching in vain,
In case another goes off again.
Dead city, trade is at rest,
Sweeping up the glass and the mess,
Workers sent home, the town is closed for the day,
And all the shoppers have gone away.

Andrew G Burton

Loner

Ancient forest cloaked by night
Drenched with diffused moonlight,
Western oceans vengeful rear
Beating waves punish rocky shore,
Star blanket over sparkling crests
Rolling breakers, heaving chests,
Solitary figure shrouded in black
Roams lonely, writhing forest track,
Route familiar in sadness caped
Eerie figure in mystery draped,
Summoned by ghostly voices drifting
Sands of time forever shifting,
Cries of comrades, lovers lost
Such a punishment, terrible cost,
Harbouring no fear but crippling pain
Cold, dark night, flickering flame,
Sounds of forest connotes home
Treads where most fear to roam,
Lonely warrior abroad by night
Searching for the ultimate fight.

Jonathan Frank Tate

My Land of Beauty

It's beautiful this land of Wales
With craggy nooks along the Dales,
The hills we climb are mighty high,
They almost reach up to the sky,
I feel the breeze flow through my hair,
And smell the freshness in the air,
My dog has come along as well,
She likes the walks, for I can tell,
Her tail keeps wagging to and fro,
While farmers harvest with their sow,
Her name is Bess, my little girl,
She's ageing now, my bonnie pearl,
Then up and on we climb again,
Through all the winds and pouring rain,
We stride through fields of golden corn,
And watched as lambs were being born,
They jumped about so full of glee,
Like showing off to Bess and me,
We crossed a style that's on the farm,
Where everything was nice and calm,
Then later on we crossed a brook,
Where I took out my Holy Book,
From far away, the church bells rang,
And listened as the choir sang,
Come on my pet, I said to Bess,
Today's been full of happiness,
So all of you who walk the Vales,
Are welcome to this land of Wales.

Griffith Owen Roberts

Childhood

I see the child at play today
And mind rolls back in memory.
To skipping rope, hopscotch game
Rows of houses, all the same,
But everybody knows my name.
A quiet street, gas lamps tall
Cast friendly light on me, so small
A 'cosy' shop with bacon sliced
wrapped in greaseproof paper white
Sweets in jars, colourful, bright.
A penny apple, sheer delight.
Hide and seek in entry dark
A game of cricket in the park.
I see the child, different, I know
Computer games and video,
Yet in my heart I have to say
Please may he know the joy of play.

Shirley Smith

I Married a Tiger and Had my Face Scratched

Low through the jungle, she stalked her way
From her face, her intentions, I could not say
First a low purr, and the soft padded paw
When in the jungle, you must follow the law.

The heat of the night, began to tell on me
This was my last chance to ever break free
I opened my eyes and looked into the night
And that's when I got the most terrible fright

Close to my side and snug in the bed
There was a tiger next to my head
I swallowed hard and then dared to look
It could have been a tale from Jungle Book

I blinked my eyes and got the shock of my life
It wasn't a tiger, but my wife
Calmed and relaxed, I told of my nightmare
But all she would do was sit and stare

I ran for the door, at a quick pace
Then felt a huge claw scrape down my face
I got to the door, and it was latched
I've married a tiger and had my face scratched.

C Christison

The Countryside

Down country lanes you see so much
the little hedge sparrows the lovely song thrush
A cuckoo call or at night an owl
the sly old fox who is on the prowl
Rabbits popping up from burrowed holes
underground the burrowing moles
Honeysuckle that smells so sweet
the wildest of flowers both pretty and neat
Far away from the busy roads
leaping about are fat old toads
Twinkling dewdrops at daybreak
the smell of new mown hay
Night moths find a place to rest
butterflies come to play
The countryside is bountiful
it holds wondrous things
A gift to each and everyone
who loves the natural things.

Patricia Barr

Guarded

Transparent fronts
Through which we peek
Resolve to keep our hearts disguised;
And cloaked in truth,
The lies we tell
Attempt to feign an innocence.

With open eyes
That will not see,
We promise hearts too freely given.
Audition love;
You play my part,
For I would break these roles you've cast.

S Louise Allan

Widow's Weeds

Mary had a little fault
She liked a quiet puff.
Now, everyone was telling her
That she had smoked enough.

It followed her to work one day
'No smoking any more'
They caught her taking 'just a drag'
And she was shown the door.

Mary was a kindly soul
Her pleasures minimal
Suddenly it seemed that she'd
Become a criminal.

The comfort of that cigarette
She never dreamt - provoking!
Until she heard the media
Assault on passive smoking.

Determined then to play her part
She went for one last pack
A farewell gesture to her 'love'
She never made it back.

Her dying wish - a cigarette
As medic knelt beside her
A final gasp and she was gone
Not nicotine - *Joyrider*!

D M Hargreaves

A Suffolk Green

The dew has kissed the village green
Like diamonds cast from heaven
An oak tree reaches for the skies.
Its memories forbidden.
Pigeons explode from its branches like fireworks
on the fifth.
A thousand pennies in the well.
I wish, I wish, I wish,
Young children chasing butterflies they have
No hope of catching, the silence of this
Virgin morn is broken by their laughing
A golden sun pours all its warmth
On everything it's seen, this is to me a
Memory of a Suffolk village green.

L Parker

Boredom

Mum is in the garden,
Dad is making tea
Everyone is busy,
All except for me!

Brother's in the pantry,
Sisters in their room.
No-one seems to notice me,
They've forgotten me, I assume.

I stand around, just watching,
I'm told I'm in the way.
I think I shall go crackers,
Oh, what a boring day!

Kay Rimmington (12)

Untitled

Man said
I made what I called a super ship
She sailed the oceans far and near
And braved raging storms without a fear.

God said
I made a little duckling very small
Which did not seek the world beyond
But swam with joy, the village pond.

Man said
I can paint all the things which I see
The sunset and dawn the mountains so high
Flowers and trees and birds in the sky.

God said
Do not forget that I made this world
Gave you the beauty you can find there
And all its sweet treasures which you share.

Man said
A clever mind is all that I need
These old simple truths are not for me
When all these new wonders here I see.

God said
I gave you knowledge for you to decide
How my truths bring peace beyond compare
The ways of the world will bring despair.

May Walker

In Our Little House in a Back Street

In our little house in a back street
The folks there are devine
They mind each other's kids you know
When each one goes to town
They send around for fish and chips
And pop and ice-cream too
They give you lumps of bread and jam
Free soap and water too
The kids all gather round the room
Have fun and laughter too
It's quite a night on a Saturday night
With thirty or forty too
In our little house in a back street
The fun we have you'd be surprised
Goes on 'til half past two
There's Joe with all the saucepan lids
And Bill with trays of spoons
And Gert with all her curlers in
And Granny looking blue
These kids are happy so who cares
In our little house in a back street.

H B Mitchell

Perception

Birds in raincoats eating ice-cream
Called my son when three years old.
We saw starlings peck through hoar frost.
Sleek survivors, lively, bold.

Now us in raincoats with our ice-cream,
With gulls and starfish by the sea.
Birds with bibs on have a foam bath,
Shouted grandson, full of glee.

In thirty years between those moments,
My rings grew tight, then loosed again.
Hard days assuaged by childrens' vision,
Their antidote to loss and pain.

J McDonald

The Compromise of Life

The mighty oak stood straight and tall,
Before I was a boy,
And, in its branches I recall,
Sweet memories of joy.
But round its base, the roots were rung,
With common nettles, and they stung.

And tho' each year I cut them low,
Each year again they grew,
Until 'twas time for me to go,
And start a life anew,
Another time, another face, in destiny to take my place.

In later years, I heard them tell,
Of how the mighty tree,
Had, in the storms and tempest fell,
And all I now could see,
Around the stump, where once it grew,
A host of stinging nettles new.

And so this little verse I end,
The moral clear to all,
If, to the storms of life we bend,
There is no need to fall -
But like the nettles, rise again -
To conquer hardship, fear, and pain.

D K Brough

Compromise

I've tried to write a novel
But I haven't got the knack,
I produced a few short stories
But they all kept coming back,
I thought about whodunits
But I hadn't got a clue.

So I wrote for television,
But the scripts just wouldn't do,
I pinned my hopes on drama,
That did not do the trick,
And my sweet romantic poetry
Made even me feel sick
So I finally decided
Since I can't do any better,
To give up the impossible
And simply write a letter.

Norma Pass

Spring

Trees are heavy with blossom
Bumble bees out on a spree
It has been such a long long winter
Now there is so much to see

Lilac tree dressed in palest green
Hark how the blackbird sings
Search for the delicate primrose
What frail, sweet, fragile things

There goes the very first swallow
Spring now really is here
Back from their winter vacation
To bring us such beauty and cheer

April and May the loveliest time
When the earth awakes from its sleep.
Can anyone doubt on seeing all this?
There really *is* life after death.

J Hickens

Half an Eye

When looking around to see, what you see
Take a good look, and see, and see.
Don't look with only half measure,
There are things out there, to see and
treasure.
The sway of the trees, the trill of the
birds
The hedgerows that guard the cows in
their herds
Flowers that bloom in gay abandon
Scattering their seeds to the wind at
random.
Take a good look, with not half an eye
Out there, there is much to espy.
A rabbit that scurries along the way,
Tomorrow he may, be someone's prey.
A mouse or a mole, with whiskers
twitching,
He stops to scratch, because he is
itching.
A sky that is clear and blue
Gives joy to me and you.
The grass, a lovely shade of green
These gifts, must be treasured when seen.
This is the reason, I'm telling you why
Do not look, with half an eye.

N Stokes

The West Midlands

West Midlands home of my heart.
Never have I yearned to part.
Place where I was born and bred
District where I will live 'til dead.

Our great conglomeration has it all,
From Spaghetti Junction to great football.
An indoor Arena that beats the world,
To orchestras and opera that all applaud.

An industrial giant since the war,
Multi-skilled tradesmen and so much more.
Foreigners arrived from over the seas,
All have settled and feel at ease.

Car manufacture is our forte,
Industries built around the four wheel wonder.
Yet never forget our other expertise and skills,
From Aero-space metals to rolling mills.

Years of profit, growth and boom,
Then into decline with recessionary gloom.
The giant is awakening from its demise
Industrial barometer for all mankind.

Always the centre of political intrigue,
Governments key to the Parliamentary door!
Yet not deceptable to their lies and misdeeds,
A community when speaks all takes heed.

Many great cities, cathedrals and towns,
The heart of England beating proud.
Oh how I love this wondrous stage,
The lands, the rivers and its heritage.

John A Walsh

Summer

How many times have I been kissed by the sun
In these hazy days, long ago before now?
Hazy, lazy days, when my world forgets to turn
And time doesn't know about forever.

But the sun -
Its long fingers have reached down to me,
And I too have reached up and held its golden, eternal hands
as I bathed in its mother shaped arms.
But who will keep these golden days turning when I'm
old enough to die?

And who will watch the gentle willow weep
and silently weep too for her sadness.
Yes! - many times have I been kissed by the sun,
but may I ask that when my time comes,
I can reach up for one last time,
and kiss the sun goodbye.

J Taylor

Books

Clean ones, grubby ones
On the library shelves
Tatty ones, dog eared ones
We can help ourselves.

Taking us to far off places
Into other realms
Reading of other races
From the library shelves.

Where would we be without them,
Not to be able to read,
About other people from all walks of life,
Books on the library shelves.

Open a book and the story unfolds,
As we sit engrossed by the hour.
A story which our attention holds.
All on the library shelves.

F M Collins

The Englishman

I am just one of the Englishmen,
Was born in the land of the free;
And that makes us patriotic then,
When born in the land of the free.

They can never put out the sunlight,
Or darken the light of the rays;
Others can try with all of their might,
But they will never change our ways.

From far off lands the valiants come
To upset the ones who are free;
But we shall stand and we shall not run,
For we shall never bend the knee.

And if you can stop the tide that turns
Or end the water in the sea;
Then you will know just why the world turns,
And the ways of birds in a tree.

From over the world they come and when
Should they try to change you and me?
We are just the funny Englishmen,
That's why we shall always be free.

Dennis Parkes

Bread to Share

His coat was thin shabby and worn
Wrapped around his shoulders a scarf that was torn
Not very cosy for a cold winter's morn'.

His boots were old and down at the heel,
If he were our brother how would we feel,
An old woolly hat, holes in his gloves,
Shuffling along the best he could,
Helped with a stick covered with mud.

He murmured 'Good Morning' as I passed by,
A lost look on his face, a tired look in his eyes,
Clutched in his hand a thick piece of bread,
I wondered if ever he would find a warm bed.

Over his shoulder he carried a sack,
Were his worldly possessions in that,
How does a poor soul survive is it too much to ask.

A sad voice called with concern, 'Where are you Rob?'
There was his friend a little black dog,
The dog wagged his tail, looked up to his face,
The tramp shared his bread with his little mate,
Off they walked, disappearing from sight,
I pray they will find a warm shelter tonight.

M N Roan

Old Summer

Bright, white sunshine floods
The jade-green carpet of the summer meadow,
And the eternal, beckoning blue
Hugs the horizon in every direction.

Seeds of the woodland flowers
Lift and fall on the cooling westerly breeze
As a flock of black swans whistle above me
On their way to another continent.

My shadow hides beneath my feet
The air begins to still
And July's warm cloak closes around me
As the sun glides to its highest point.

This is England's summertime
The melodic buzz of the busy bumble bee
The broad-leaved oak trees in the wood
All of this, hidden away, in my fading memory.

Richard Swainson

The Vixen an Encounter

With faltering steps at last she came,
Her fragile body torn with pain,
With dim and almost sightless eyes,
She stared around.
I put the food I had prepared upon the ground.

She turned her suffering eyes to me,
Then so clearly I could see,
The cause of all her misery,
Dear God, this wondrous being whom you had made,
Now by humankind, made so afraid,
By monstrous cruelty, hugely laid.
She turned in hopeless sad retreat,
And did not dare to stay to eat.

Dear Lord, the very earth did reel,
And to my soul, cold guilt did steal.

Joe Hodgkinson

Untitled

I saw the trees
A-dancing, a-dancing, a-dancing
I saw the trees a-dancing
A-dancing in the breeze

Their dress of green
Was swirling, was swirling, was swirling
To gather all the sunshine
For summer days were here

Once more I saw the trees
A-dancing, a-dancing
But now their dress
Was green and gold
For autumn had its sway

No more I saw the trees
A-dancing, a-dancing
For winter with its icy grip
Had stole their hearts away

But once again I saw the trees
A-dancing, a-dancing
For spring had come
Oh joy of joys
Once more in green array.

G M Jones

Me!

My thoughts and dreams transcended,
The cage that my mind is in,
They leak into my skin,
So I always know they live.
The strength of my endurance,
The essence of my pain,
The coldness of my tears,
The fire within my veins,
Black tribals war dancing,
The darkness that I feel,
But colour surrenders some light,
Making them real,
And finally the beginning,
Wrought from my pain,
The bird and flower fighting,
And innocence is lost again.

C J Brookes

Job in Prospect?

People were sitting
Waiting in a room.
Waiting their turn for
A job interview.
Someone struck a match
Lit a cigarette.
Just to pass the time,
Staring into space.
Some chatted and laughed,
Easing the tension.
Others stared, pondered,
Wondered would it be
So, their lucky day.
Crossing their arms, legs,
Fingers twitching,
Clicking nervously.
In their hands, a form
For job application.

John Selby

Maybe

'We'll do so-and-so next year,' they said gaily
'Or the year after,' then added, 'maybe.'
The years flew by relentlessly,
So busy were they, they didn't see
They should have paused, the hour to savour,
Tasted life's joys, and enjoyed the flavour
Of all the happy hours they shared.
Then they would have been well prepared
For that dread moment, when all alone
They faced the future; without a moan,
Without regrets, with no 'if onlys' to appall,
But thankful for fond memories to recall.

Joan Perry

My Tortoise

I'd like to write an ode about my tortoise
But there isn't really much that one can say,
He's not a cause for any great excitement
As he wanders in my garden every day.

I wonder, does he wish that he was different
Does he wish that he could shed his tiresome shell
And jump and fly into the tree tops
Alas, he cannot speak, so who can tell.

As he lumbers up the path so very slowly
To take a piece of lettuce from hand,
There is no sign of pleasure or emotion
If he could wag a tail, that would be grand.

His little face devoid of all expression
Is he happy, is he sad, one cannot tell,
If he could make some sign, some gesture
To me know he's fit and all is well.

I cannot stroke or nurse him like a kitten
And tell him that I love him, that I care,
But I think he knows he has my fond affection
For he always comes to greet me when I'm there.

I think that he could teach us all a lesson,
To reach a goal however hard the way
Just plod along with grim determination
Like tortoise, you will get there, come what may.

F Elkington

War

'War is pointless, and stupid',
Let's learn, to love. And play cupid,
Pains, and losses, all because,
Of too many bosses.
Senseless killing, men, children and women,
Inflicting hurt and wounds,
Just because of a difference of opinion,
and moods.
Fighting, and dying, all the time,
There's no need, it's now, we should
Tow the line.
For the good of man, me and mine,
Tears, hunger and blood,
Up to the trenches in mud,
Machine gun fire all of a blast,
Shot dead now, it's the past,
Why do we fight?
Pointless killing, someone's
husband, or someone's wife,
So precious is the gift of life,
No need to go through this war,
Don't fight with each other,
Learn to love more,
Peace and calmness,
Not alarmness,
Surely there must be happy times ahead,
Lots of jaw, not war,
Live together in harmony,
Life's for living, and you can't do that,
If you're *dead*!

Caroline Janney

Nothing's Left

Dearest mother, look at you now,
But you've survived, God only knows how,
'We'll be alright,' you used to say,
'But when mummy, when?' I hope it's today.

The cruel world, it's wars, only you knew,
I trusted the people, but most of all you,
You'd protect me, from their words, their looks,
You were so strong,
I didn't know, they knew, what was wrong.

As I got wiser, and finally grew,
I'd look at your eyes, and think, that's not you,
You'd shout and scream, batter and roar,
I would cry until I could cry no more.

Where had you gone, and what was so bad?
And why had I lost the mother I had.
No more were you gentle, generous and kind,
Instead, I'd find you, drunk, deaf and blind,
To my needs, they were no more and then,
You turned against me, your daughter and then,
I could take no more, I'd had enough,
And I finally found out that 'life was tough'.

My childhood gone, I'm sorry to say,
And still everyday, for you, I do pray,
For mummy has gone, and your bottle is dry,
And all you've got left, is time, which to die.

Richenda Williams

Untitled

Windswept seascape to the fore
Bounded by a gentle shore
Vista stretching far and wide
Timeless sands and clockwork tide.

Clouds above in mottled greys
Blending with horizon's haze
Contrast with a glinting sea
Always moving, spirit free.

Seabirds bobbing on the waves
Floating on their future graves
Others flying past in vees
Carried by a sea-fresh breeze.

Creatures free to swim and fly
Tiny specks in sea and sky
Fragile lives are Nature's norm
Living, dying in fierce storm.

Seaside breakers roar and swish
Over shoals of countless fish
Hinting of the hidden deep
Lurking in dark dreams of sleep.

Sea expressing changing mood
Taking life or giving food
Sea surrounding endless shore
Lapping sand for evermore.

Mike Franey

Believe it

You can paint as many pictures,
On canvas or in mind,
But you cannot beat reality,
In a camera's eye,
The suffering, that is happening,
Was seen on TV
And they brought back to us,
Some terrible scenes,
The starving just sit or stand,
Like sticks from barren trees,
They look as if they could snap,
Oh, so easily,
Their skin clings round their bodies,
So transparent, like cling film,
Each bone, each joint and how we are made,
Can be seen at will,
The flies are in abundance,
Chewing at the skin,
The mouth is cracked and dry,
But the real hurt is within,
The eyes tell the story,
Of pain and suffering,
If you cannot feel anything,
From what you see,
May I remain you,
It could be you or me.

Pauline Crossland

Before His Throne

One night I fell into a sleep,
so deep I began to float,
I fell deeper and deeper like in a trance,
my spirit I could not control,
My heart began to beat faster,
as a light above me I saw,
Came closer and closer to me,
my feelings I could not withdraw,
Surrounded by clouds I came closer,
and around me music flowed,
Angels around me danced,
and before me I saw a throne,
I looked into the light,
and upon the throne I saw,
A mighty King was seated,
and I stood and stared in awe,
His face shone upon me, as he looked at me with joy,
my heart was filled with comfort,
I'd never felt this loved before,
It was only in this moment, I realised I was home,
standing before my father,
Upon his heavenly throne,
And as he gazed upon me, with a look so full of pride,
I felt myself sink slowly,
back to the other side,
And as I awakened, a joy so strong within,
Made me feel so lucky, for I knew where I had been,
I really feel like I've been blessed,
and with joy I long to go,
To be with my abbah father, to stand before his throne.

Gina Whittle

The Passing

The old soldier dozed
Dreamed of wars long ago
Of uniform, rifle and pack
The muck and the blood,
The tears and the toil
And of comrades who never came back.

Through the mists of his dreams
He could see them all there
There's Harry and Jimmy and Jack
There's Charlie and Bert
And Tom what a lad
And the others who never came back.

'On Parade' was the shout
And he moved into line
His chest puffed with pride
With the band beating time
With Harry and Charlie
Tom, Jimmy and Jack
And the others who never came back.

He stood to attention
So strong in his youth
But gone long ago
"Tis a dream not the truth'
He cried in despair
But the band played on
And the boys were still there.

Norman Stephens

Market Day in the Rain

People shopping around,
People hopping around - over muddy -
Puddles shining on the ground.
It's market day, and raining cats and dogs,
And the way it's coming down -
They must be wearing clogs!
Umbrellas passing by - trying to
Poke you in the eye,
Prams and babies - toddlers too,
Crying and wailing - bump into you.
Fancy it raining, yesterday was so fine,
Summer breezes and warm sunshine.
Look at it now - cold and wet.
What's the forecast? worse to come yet!
Well I've finished shopping -
I'm off home for a cup of tea - like the rain,
I'm not stopping.

Ivy Thompson

A Mother's Thoughts

As I sit here alone
With my 'cup of tea'
I look all around
What's happened to me?

As a mother of 'twelve'
I longed for this 'peace'
The fighting, the squabbling
Would it *never* cease?

I longed for this day
For so many years.
But give me back 'my babies'
And wipe away these tears

Please busy young mums
Just look ahead
The days are soon gone
When you tuck them in bed.

Give me days if, just for a while
To cuddle my babies, and see their first smile.
If this poem seems sad as sometimes I am
I remember the 'bonus'
of being 'a Gran'.

J Thompson

A Brief Entanglement of Time

I feel I've lost you, but then, you were never mine.
Our lives crossed swiftly, in a brief entanglement of time.
A space with hidden meaning, a source of much regret.
For time is such a precious thing, this no-one should forget.
To share a drink, a meal, a laugh, all these can be replaced.
Surely time is the exception, for time is just one place.
To share a part of someone's life, if only for an hour,
Is for me a very special thing, above all other power.
So what lies in the future, to make everything feel fine.
Please God! another chance to share, a further sweet, if brief, entanglement of time.

Barbara Henry

The Beauty of Nature

If you wait 'til the sun shines
tomorrow
All around we are filled with delight.
With the flight of the birds and the
sounds to be heard all around,
Even in ditches there are riches
to be fond.
If you look for the beauty of nature,
you will find it where ever you go,
In the trees and the fields in the
hedgerows,
In each little flower that grows,
In the face of a child, in a heart that
is kind.
In our maker the creator
God of Love

Je'anne Harrison

Sands of Time

It's time to hit the road once more
Not so lonely as before
Wife and children by my side
Speak of memories just gone by
On and on we go
Through the heather through the snow
Which way shall we go
South East or West
I know which is for best
Let's rest awhile
Before we go another mile
It's time to hit the road once more
Let's follow it 'til we reach the shore
Wife and I sit holding hands
Children playing on the sands
I thought I heard a seagull cry
Or was it a call from up high
Sands of time are running out
Wife and children watch the incoming tide
They will soon be by my side
While I continue my journey to the sky

C Etheridge

Understanding

As people grow older year by year
It doesn't take much to waylay their fears
A quiet word, a gentle touch
They don't really ask for much.
Just understanding, and time to spare,
To listen a while and show we care.
Company they need as well
Someone to whom they are able to tell
Stories of their days gone by
Which bring laughter to you and I.
Their grandchildren they will always love,
The joy and laughter will help to remove
Some of the gloom which maybe they feel
Sometimes around them begins to steel.
Give to them all the love you can spare
Someday you may need a little care,
Feeling the same way as they do
Needing a bit of company too.
There is always time to continue on
With the rest of your life when they are gone.

P Martindale

Growing Pains

Babies, soft and dimpled, smiling,
Starfish hands, eyes beguiling,
Fluffy toys and bibs and rattles,
Bath time fun and teething battles.
Christmas magic, birthday joys,
Dad picking his way through the toys,
Playgroup friends and home to tea,
Then cuddled up on Daddy's knee.
A pair of brown eyes, a pair of blue,
Too soon the baby days are through.

Schooldays come with joys and sorrows,
Pals and laughs and bright tomorrows,
Brownies, Cubs and church on Sundays,
(Blue-eyes had 'school-throat' on Mondays)
Seaside holidays, treats in town,
Getting taller, strong and brown,
Brown-eyes' voice squeaks up and down,
School uniforms, chips with a dinnertime bun,
Then you know their childhood's done.

Now the house is quiet and neat.
No calling voices, no running feet.
No-one shouts, 'Mum what's for tea?'
Now there's only dad and me.
No mud, no mess, no family fun,
Now, you see, the kids have gone.

Heather Edwards

Thunderstorm at Night

A sky like ink beyond the hill,
Each living thing at rest and still.

All comes ablaze with brilliant light,
As the lightening flashes across the night.

Then clouded heavens are rent asunder,
With the echoing crash of the rolling thunder.

Swollen raindrops come dancing high,
As they lance downwards from the sky

Wild storm clouds gather, all around,
The whole earth shakes, vibrates with sound.

As if amidst the lashing rain,
Great armies clashed and fought again.

At the most fearful, trembling moments,
It seems the world is all in torment.

Man's puny efforts are put to scorn,
By the power that lives in a thunderstorm.

Soon into the distance the storm has passed,
Wild turbulence is stilled at last.

Nights shadows return, to reign supreme,
Calm is restored, all becomes serene.

James Bell

The Cactus

Banished to the garden shed
From Kitchen window sill
The thorn in the flesh of many hands
As many an '*ouch*' can tell.
Green, globular and ridged with red
Brown star shaped spikes
A cactus in a plastic pot
Which everyone dislikes.
Forgotten, neglected in the potting shed
The weeks went slowly by,
When two small hairy warts appeared
Espied by the gardener's eye.
Good Heavens! the plant is blooming,
Back to the house restored.
The petals slowly opened.
Give praise unto the Lord.
White, pale pink petals, two royal coronets,
With myriads of yellow stamens
The stigma were beset.
Ugliness like beauty is really just skin deep.
But the beauty of those flowers in my memory will keep.
Just twenty four hours they blossomed,
And then lay drooping dead!
Alas! poor ugly cactus, back to the potting shed.

Thomas Byers

A Message of Hope for Those Growing Old

As you travel steadily on life's way may you forever find - true friendship and companionship and especially peace of mind.

For contentment on life's highway is worth its weight in gold, and inward happiness and peace is a treasure to behold.

With kindness and fulfilment so gentle and serene, life is often so enriched with a quiet strength and mien.

Growing old can be a pleasure if we look with seeing eyes, forgetting our troubles, grumbles and complaints, being happy and helpful and wise.

For God Travels daily with us as on through life we go: he will not leave us helpless because he loves us so.

Although growing old, be not afraid to face what life may eventually bring: for with faith and trust in God above we can accomplish almost anything.

His steady hand has guided us throughout the pitfalls of life: he will not see us foundering on the threshold of a better life.

So with determined courage travel life's highway with an ever ready smile, for God will help and encourage you as you travel the longest mile.

Even though the odds may be against us keep travelling bravely on 'til we reach that heavenly glory and with God we are we all are one.

So travel steadfastly towards the goal we all must reach in the end as we make our peace with our God above, our maker, redeemer and friend.

Elsie Dixon

Self-Pity

Here I am. Tucked up in bed.
My nose has gone a frightful red.
First boiling hot, and now I'm freezing.
My eyes are sore. I can't stop sneezing.
My head is throbbing. Throat's on fire.
My condition is quite dire.
I've tablets, powders, flask of tea,
And Radio Four to comfort me.
Oh! What the heck. Too weak to weep.
I'll close my eyes, and go to sleep.

Mair Alexander

Untitled

As I sit here pen in hand,
I think how great life could be, how grand
if I won the pools, all that dough,
to lift me from depression and woe.
Oh how great things could be,
if I could sail across the sea,
to far off places see mystical things
to see beautiful birds with coloured wings
with kangaroos and wallabies too
and the very best doctors when I catch the 'flu.
But the greatest thing of all
is to stay in bed on a cold morn'.
Not to go out in the wind and rain
or to sit at this desk wracking my brain.
The life of luxury, that's for me.
Oh how great life would be.

Ann Aspin

When You're Old and Alone

When you're old and alone just don't despair
Or think that no-one really cares,
There's always someone planning, scheming
When you just sit alone there dreaming
You're on the list, your meal is booked
Just wonder what for you they've cooked
Your meals on wheels, they won't forget
Your home care will your table set.
She works and shops, she's very kind
You're never ever off her mind.
Friends like her when you're growing old
Are really to you, more precious that gold
But, beware, if there's a knock at the door,
There are rogues, that have bad plans in store
Ask for their card, if there's any doubt.
Just lock the door and keep them out
When there are things you cannot do
Just think, there are others far worse off than you
Just close your eyes, and say a prayer
For God is always waiting there
You're never alone, He's by your side,
If you will let Him be your guide
Pray Heavenly Father up above,
Send your angels with your love.
To grant you grace accept your pardon
And take you to rest in His heavenly garden.

Kathleen Heyden Dale

For Rachel on Her 90th Birthday

In nineteen thirty four we met
Two neighbours very new
And I was twenty three
And you were thirty two.

These were very lean years
The days of make do and mend
And although we hadn't much money
At least we had a friend.

Now today is your ninetieth birthday
And I thought I'd like to mark it
By buying you a brand new car
But I know you'd nowhere to park it.

So I thought of a diamond ring
Or perhaps a golden locket
But then I had to admit
They didn't suit my pocket.

And finally I came to flowers
A modest sweet nosegay
I know they are always welcome
And would affectionately convey
My loving thoughts and prayers for you
On this your special day.

Margaret Brownless

The Smile of God

As ferns unfold there's strands of green,
And flowers upturn to greet the sun,
The burnished corn, a golden flood
Prompts mankind to praise his God.

The trees and bushes awake at dawn,
And winged creatures fill the air,
All nature seems to greet the morn'
For life is good, as it is fair.

And yet . . . and yet, the anguished cry
Of hungry children fill the ear,
How long can we, when thanking God . . .
Filled with plenty, fail to hear . . .

Dennis Stiff

Untitled

In pristine wards
their white skirts shine
as about their business they do stride
with cheerful mien and watchful eye
over their charges they preside

Dependant on them for all their care
their charges feel secure
as with professional zeal
their duties they discharge

Angels of the ward they are
but humans ne'er the less
with feelings of joy or sorrow
like all they will confess
but hide the hurt, dismiss the pain
to heal the sick and aid the dying
with cheer for everyone.

Neil Pearson

Out of my Depth

Strength combating density,
I crest the cool caress of waves,
And looking down,
I see the blue dune landscape fall away.
But now I glide too far,
And guiding landscape landmarks disappear.
Swelling movement starts to chill me through
And fear of unseen fingers
Clutching at my flailing limbs,
Morbid long dead sea men
Look to me to rescue them,
Or pull me under with them
To a silent world of distant light,
Merging with compressing, starless night.

John Tirebuck

One Day

An old man in a wheelchair
said to me one day
Come a little closer
Don't stand so far away

A blind man on a bus
Asked me the time of day
So I told him
But gave nothing else away

A man took my hand
And held it tight
Now I think of him
Night after night

I feel I am lost
Never to be found
Seems the only peace I'll find
Is underground.

V Elmer

Jesus

Endless would be the night,
but for His bright light.
A beacon on high,
beckons all who will try.

A prayer or two,
from me and you.
Let Him know we're there,
that we haven't despaired.

His pain and torment,
is mankind's lament.
Let's never forget,
or make Him regret.

He said He'd forgive,
if we learn to live.
Lives peaceful and sharing,
make life worth Him caring.

Mark Sims

Atoms

Atoms, electrons neutrons
are just a name to me
of some mystical, mysterious being,
an uncertain, concealed secret
wrapped in a parcel
of ignorance.

I want to trust the few
who know all these secrets
of atoms, electrons and neutrons -
I want to pacify my doubts
that they will use
their knowledge
without hatred and abuse.

But how can I dismiss the doubts
that creep into my mind:
how can I turn a blind
eye when I know
that the secrets of science
can leak and flow:
they can sow
seeds of suspicion.

But I must trust
those who possess
the secrets:
I must thrust
all mistrust
from my mind.

Peace and trust
walk hand in hand;
when I know peace
I know trust;
when I know trust
I know peace.

Margaret Emlyn Jenkins

Deceased

I tread the grass towards your grave,
Unsure of how I should behave.
Do I laugh or weep with grief?
Shall I throw or place this wreath?

I cast my glance across your place -
And I still see your evil face;
Do I kneel to pay respect?
Shall I gloat and stand erect?

I read the script above your head,
No mention of the hate you bred.
Loving words, that don't make sense -
Adding to the old pretence.

And now a stone is your disguise
That stands between my truth - your lies.
How could you plot to build my trust?
Then gratify your selfish lust?

Now I'm on trial as the accused -
They won't believe that you abused.
Will my handcuffs be released?
Is my soul, with you - deceased?

Caroline Furlong

Bygone Days

Emotion wells up as I recall bygone days,
Happiness at a sweet remembered thought.
Family singalongs around the piano sung,
Memories such as these can't be bought.

I wish I could grasp at bygone days,
Then I would have my beloved dog Bill,
Who'd I'd cuddle so tight, when I was afraid,
I yearn for my dear friend still.

A tear in my eye begins to creep,
As I think of a dear and treasured friend.
I remember all the tears and joys we shared,
And how our friendship would never end.

I always felt growing up seemed so hard,
But being grown is harder still.
To be young, an innocent once again,
Would be my one delight and thrill.

Oh! For the chance to begin all again,
Righting the wrongs that were done;
To experience life, try pastures new,
Delight at knowing the battle was won.

Delight at knowing you'd done it all right,
Lived life to the full - and fought the good fight.
'But life's never perfect,' I think as I sigh,
Though I still love to dream of times gone by.

Linda Slade

Three Wishes

Soft, gentle, I saw the snow fall.
Loud and clear, I heard the robin call.
The boughs of holly hanging in the hall.
A Christmas tree so green and tall.
Snugly lies a baby in his manger stall.
Three wishes of peace, joy and love to all.
Three simple words so easy to recall.
Are forgotten! Because man needs to destroy all.

Norma Tate

Shop Soiled

A sigh, a throb, that's what I was,
A Grand Mal, yes - an ache obeyed,
a fleeting feeling, jailed in flesh,
a butterfly, crucified, winced on its pin;

You were an emotional spasm,
a curdled, sour, orgasm,
sixteen years of grief -
the calendar on fire, the clock repenting;

Shop-soiled, wrong gift in an odd box,
substandard, not to spec, unable to be changed,
A drop of bloody drink too much,
The moon too bright, the whole night

drowned in wine, swimming in her perfume;
I had such plans for you, God knows, I tried -
You could have been -

I could have been your best possession,
matched the house, blended with the car;
Why didn't you wallpaper over me?

I married (for appearance sake), saved up
to buy her, and your love, to get -

to get respect, yes; but I was just
a tidal wave that swept the bed,
couldn't be held back, or else your soul,
blistering, black, would have exploded
in sheets of flame; so here I sit -

In my hall of mirrors, shattered,
with you sucking juices from me,
food for your Dracula soul; must dash,
nothing personal, my life is waiting,

to go on, within me, without you - Goodbye!

Richard Westall

Untitled

I have cleaned your house,
I have cooked your food
I gave you all my love,
but it's done me no good.

You're out every night,
getting drunk having fights.
And you never come home on time.
So my dear husband,
I really must say
This is where I draw the line.

I have found a flat and a very good job,
I need no longer live
with a fat drunken slob!
I have been asleep for far too long.
I am now wide awake
and from you I have gone.

Michelle Irving

Dog-Free Beaches

No more on our favourite summer beach
Will he dash to find hidden caves
Or weave his way to unmarked balls,
Friendly children and white furled waves.
Then shake a million sandy sea-drops
On my well-oiled sun-baked body
As he smiles with sparkling rapture
During innocent escapes.
Under my stripy canvas chair
No dozing mongrel lying there
With wriggling toes that dance in dreams
Of buried spades and licked ice-creams.
And when the wicker hamper creaks
No dripping tongue and melting eyes
Feigned indifference or mock surprise
To welcome our salty picnic.
Or stolen visits to the shore
My thoughts are with him left behind
And as we bask in summer sun
He wanders gently through my mind.
At home our tell-tale trail of sand
For him it's hard to understand
Yet still he wags his drooping tail
As he slowly comes to greet us.

Carol Woodford

Four Legged Friend

My four legged friend
Was a friend to the end
He gave me years of pleasure
I remember when he was small
He used to climb the trees so tall
Then as he got old
He was not so bold
But I thought he would live for ever
Sadly that was not to be
Now he is buried under that tree
But I still see him
Coming through the door
Saying meow meow meow
Once more.

Lillian Leigh

The Industrial Revolution

The industrial revolution, brought happiness it seemed,
if we could have seen the future, we would have had different
dreams,

everyone looked on as unemployment was created,
now we are confronted, by a nation, so frustrated.

The get rich schemes, have left the planet, in such a sorry state,
look at our nation now, most wanting to emigrate,
we must protect our planet, before it surely dies,
in our strife on land now, and in the skies.

Wars are taking place, all for the greed of man,
nation against nation, all for the sake of land.
overpopulation, is one cause of so much stress,
we must look at our future breeding habits,
with policies, now to address.

The world, is on a destructive path, and now has come the time,

to change the world we live in, and give each other,

Peace of mind.

Stephen T Maslen

Contemporary South West

How can we adequately describe
The beauteous South West countryside
The glory of its country towns
The quaint old hamlets still around?

Dartmoor with its wild expanse
Of solitude and silence to entrance
Clothed in bracken, scrub and gorse
Embellished with eroded tors.

Exmoor again with its wide expanse
Where the wild ponies frisk and prance
Where the hills are purply blue
Heather paints them a delightful hue.

In Cornwall too the tin mines see
An industry gone it seems to me
But see the white mounds of china clay
Still exported to lands far away.

Towns and villages are worth more than a glance
The churches and castles their prestige enhance
The shops - the old and the new
Receive you with smiles and bid you adieu.

But there's a change in the market place
The shoppers wear a longer face
So many folk with nothing to do
And money short - there's an air of gloom.

In village and town the plight's there to see
'House for sale' boards saying please buy me
Let's hope green shoots will now reappear
To give these South Westers their much needed cheer.

Dennis G Skirton

Memorable Year at Holbeach College

Being a girl of remarkable courage
was my one and only advantage
striving incessantly increasing in confidence
performing to others with great evidence
intense knowledge justified them all
knocked senseless and made them a fool
Hoodwinked is more like an answer
It happened by chance in one great venture
Lecturers stunned in amazement
staggering with such astonishment
All recommend me with credit
clarifying to others I had proved it
A prize I acquired for achieving success
Having dedication and worthiness
I infer I was relatively vivacious
incremented my power in being propitious
I adored a dispute on few subjects
listened to lecturers discussing their projects
I am one committed to history
reporting news and telling my story
Students disinterested in many affairs
only myself had the strong awares
never were they on the prospective
I was smart, always on the receptive
I'll always refer to the happy times I had
gave people curiosity, now they're glad
with advanced knowledge and advice I took
My highbrow understandings I now write a book.

Sarah Whitehead

The Waveney Valley

The favourite part of the river for me,
At Shotford Bridge it flows,
The mill stream, the flowers, the birds that sing,
On and on it goes.

At Mendham by the bridge, it's wide,
An ugly bridge I fear,
The Waveney passes underneath
But folk are pleasant here.

From Mendham it meanders on,
Not seen much from the road,
On Suffolk side, by Target hill,
To Homersfield takes its load.

Down beyond Flixton, over the fen,
Passing by the farm,
Bringing swans from Homersfield,
Leaving 'The Black Swan' charm.

Through Earsham wolds, where fishes swim,
Over sandy bottomed bays,
Where Bungay ladies walk their dogs,
And freisian cows malaise.

O'er Suffolk marshes soft and green,
The Waveney winds its way,
It circles around the common,
Where earnest golfers play.

Two lovely counties it divides,
Between Suffolk and Norfolk to roam,
Bungay in a horseshoe stands
Waveney Valley is its home.

Jan Rusted

My Shopping Spree in Thirty Three

My shopping spree in
'Thirty three'
Armed with cash a pound
or more,
I made a dash to the
grocer's store.

When in I got and looked
around
for my Sunday lunch
quite soon I
found.

'Can I help you?' the
grocer said,
'Oh yes,' said I, 'two
pounds of ham
and a loaf of bread.
I think I'll have
a jar of jam.'

The grocer said, 'Will
that be all?'
with a kindly grin,
'Yes,' I said. 'Just
for today,
I'll call again
when I come in.'

'How much is this I've
bought today?'
'Just half a crown,
Thank you Miss,
Bye, bye for now.'

George Ponting

St Valentine's Day - 1986

Fourteenth of February.
Then why so sad?
Memories cling
Of gallant friends departed. Sing
Dona eis requiem.

In the firelight
Winter shadows.

Memory hears
Valentines of the boisterous years.
Dona eis requiem.

recorded music softly sings
Mozart's Lacrimosa rings.
'Golden lads and lasses must . . .'
But God - life has no room for rust.
Dona nobis pacem.

Nita Nicholson

Too Old to Fight?

My Father's great indignity, in nineteen thirty nine,
Was being told he's no more use to fight upon the line.
He wanted so to volunteer to venture out to sea,
As he had done in World War One, but now they hissed 'senility!'

'Senility?' my Father roared, more angered than offended,
' 'Twas men like me, last time around, that saw the battle ended.
We didn't flinch, like pink-faced maids, who might have been
affrighted,
But stood our ground, while all around fell shattered and benighted.'

The Board of aged Admirals, all wrinkled, deaf and blind,
Had gazed upon my Pater's stance, from which they were inclined
To judge him frail for battle, and though his will was keen,
They did not feel this man of steel upon a bridge should lean.

'Twas true he'd done his duty, and had fought a battle fine,
His little ship, though overpowered, had stood its place in line.
They'd sunk the mighty enemy, and lived to tell the tale.
The Old Man knew they were the few who'd blazed the holy trail.

But still they could condemn him, to stay at home and pine,
They knew he longed to be out there, a-battling on the brine.
At forty-eight they told him, 'No! Your place is by the fire.
A man your age, near Life's Last Page - you really should retire!'

He looked along the lines of faces, purple from the port
They'd taken in through many years, and gave a mighty snort!
'What are you cretins saying?' - forgetting rank and place -
For Admirals all, in that great hall, were near the Day of Grace!

Not one was under eighty years, and Great-grandfathers all,
And yet they viewed my Father, and had the bloody gall
To tell him he's 'too old to fight, and better off in bed.
So leave the War, and all its gore - to men like us instead!'

Brian Courtman Churcher

War

War is such a bitter thing
full of death and pain
I'd like to know why they fight
Because in the end what do they gain.
Missiles flying here and there
and people running everywhere
All the people that we all loved
Go to God up above
War means death in another word
which I think we've all heard
You can lose an arm you can lose a leg
Thank God you die if you lose your head
Bombs and grenades go bang in the air
Didn't I tell you that war's not fair.

Joanne Burgess

Why

Why oh why has it got to be
When all around the world we see
Are people who are hungry, people who are sad
Many a poor soul has lost all they ever had
The suffering in Bosnia should never never be
It makes me really wonder how evil man can be
Where little children suffer, they're maimed and some can't see
They have to suffer the rest of their lives and they're innocent you see
Then there are those who go planting bombs without a thought or a care
They're evil, they're heartless yet human beings too.
In fact they really look just like me or you.
Then there are those with nowhere to live, nowhere to call their own
There are muggers and joyriders and burglars as well
Who really make other people's lives hell
Then there are those who would lay down their lives
In fact they'd do anything to stop this strife
This world of ours is a beautiful place if only people would see
The beauty all around us the sun, the moon, the sea
If only people would listen, if only people would care
If only everyone would kneel and say their prayers
Then listen to the Lord above, listen then learn to live with love.

Olga Giblin

Summer Flowers

In the park the breeze stirs
The flowers to nod their heads
Towards the summer sun.

Other flowers breeze by,
Showing what they have to offer
To the males of their species.

The males nod their heads
In appreciation,
A buzz of conversation
As they discuss the finer points
That makes the perfect flower.

In great detail they discuss
The colour, the shape, the size,
Their dress, how short, how tall,
How they move, in the summer sun.

Then the male advances on
Its particular flower,
With all the fine points that,
That male believes,
Makes a perfect flower.

He approaches, he thinks
He is the bee's knees to
All: not a thought what
The flower may think of him.

Brian Victor Walker

The Storm

Outside the thunder is roaring,
Pitter patter the rain is pouring,
A flash from the lightning,
A crash from a tree,
The wind is so strong
There are no birds singing their songs,
The rain is beating against the ground,
There are so many different sounds.
The wind sounds lonely just like me,
There's nothing much outside to see,
The trees are bowing,
The wind is howling,
The clouds are grey,
I just have to say,
The storm today is bad,
Bad bad bad.

Kelly Thorne (10)

A Brilliant Treasure

And what is this life,
That makes an offering
Too long for the suffering -
Too short for the content?
Show me the man
Who claims his hold to everything,
And I will see the hands, the empty hands,
Of a heart of void.

Innocence -
She owns the world.
Free from the pangs of undiscipled love.
Free from the corruption of industrial sloth.
Yes,
She wears a crown discoloured not by smog,
For it is the one that lacks true nurture.

As the stranger passes by,
Ignoring the music she leaves in the shrubbery,
Asking for those with the ears to listen.
As the grass tastes the sweet melody,
Of a passing breath,
Belonging to the dew of a morning's kiss, gone by.

Hold on to the tongue,
As a complaint yields its fingerprint,
Into an air -
It is not worthy.

The thoughts satisfy themselves
And leave the neighbour none the wiser.

Dean Potter

Reflection

Through still night a beacon gleams,
Reflecting, aye a thousand dreams,
A memory, a passing thought,
Of someone surely Heaven taught,
A fleeting glimpse that's all maybe,
A tender look, a yen to see,
Shining head bent low in task,
Seems but to me that's all I ask,
And so thoughts wander on and on,
'Til journey's end should keep us one,
For one alone seems so remote,
Like glassy sea with upturned boat,
So let it be as in a dream,
A thousand memories for my requiem.

G Smith